Ben Carson: Gifted Hands for a More Perfect Union

Michael Joshua

ISBN-13: 978-1519109354
ISBN-10: 1519109350

DEDICATION

This book is dedicated to all those interested in the political candidates running for the US Presidency in 2016.

CONTENTS

ACKNOWLEDGMENTS

At the time this book was written, Ben Carson was running for President. I tried to put this book together to present Ben Carson's side on all the main topic issues that the Presidential candidates are asked during the debates. Whether you have been following the debates or not, Ben Carson is an interesting man to research. My hopes is that this book will provide you with a very high-level view on the man, his past, his views, and how he turned from doctor to Presidential candidate.

1 INTRODUCTION

If anyone had told Ben Carson when he was a young boy that he would be running for president in 2015, he probably would have said that they were crazy. At the age of sixty four, Carson has lived a long enough life to see what can benefit this country. He's lived through countless Presidents and lived through a few wars. He knows what works and what doesn't work when it comes to running a country.

While some might say that his age is perfect for the presidency, others might say that might mean his policies are outdated. Carson has certainly changed his views over time to fit with the times, but whether or not those views connect with today's youth is debatable.

President of the United States is quite a feat to strive for, especially when you've had no political experience like Carson. What he lacks in experience, he makes up for in drive and in his public speaking skills. If you are a good public speaker, then it will be much easier to sway than crowds than if you are a meek, unconvincing speaker.

When Ben was young, he wanted to be a physician. He did not really have any dreams of becoming a politician while he was attending primary school. In fact, he actually had terrible grades during his first few years in school. However, due to his mother's constant perseverance and love of reading, Ben really started to appreciate just how much he could learn from the world.

Living in poverty didn't make Ben any less inclined to bring his grades up. Although he helped his mom with chores around the house, he was never forced to go out and get a job. His education came first.

Ben began to read a lot more and soon enough, his grades increased dramatically. He gained knowledge from all across the board and started a life long journey in pursuit of learning. In high school, Ben was one of the best in his class and after he graduated with honors, he went on to attend Yale University. A boy who thought he had no promise grew up to be a student who was admitted to Yale University. Through reading, Carson learned that anything is possible.

Throughout Carson's early life, he identified as a democrat. It wasn't until he was introduced to Ronald Reagan that he realized just how much he identified with the Republican Party. From then on, he became a conservative and called himself a Republican.

He claims that his eyes were opened when he saw Reagan rise to the top because before Reagan, he agreed with Democratic policies that he would never admit to agreeing with today. Carson is a prime example of how people can grow and change over time. As people become older, their tendencies toward certain policies and ideas change and with it, so does their frame of mind.

2 COLLEGE LIFE

Yale University was the true beginning of Ben Carson's life. He was determined to become a physician and get out of college with a good degree. He obtained a degree in psychology from Yale and went on to graduate studies at the Medical School of the University of Michigan.

It was here that he decided psychiatry was not the chosen path for him. Instead, he realized his aptitude for neurosurgery. Not only did he have a keen eye, but his hand-eye coordination skills were especially excellent. These attributes made him a top candidate to become a neurosurgeon.

He excelled in medical school and went on to become a neurosurgery resident at the Johns Hopkins Hospital in Baltimore, Maryland. Over the next few years, he would work and study at this hospital until he eventually became a pediatric neurosurgeon director there. He accomplished this feat at age thirty two, showing just how long it took for him to master his discipline.

He was considered to be the best surgeon at the hospital, which is why he was promoted to the position of director at such a young age. Generally, directors were older because they had more experience, but Carson did his job so well that the hospital believed he could handle the job.

3 THE BEGINNING

Over the course of his time at Johns Hopkins, Carson accomplished many things. He focused on the separation of craniopagus (Siamese) twins while working as the Director of Pediatric Neurosurgery. He separated his first pair of twins, the Binder twins, in 1987. They were joined at the back of the head, which was one of the hardest Siamese twin separation procedures. Most of the time, this procedure failed and at least one of the infants always died, but Dr. Carson agreed to take on the surgery regardless.

With a surgical team of seventy people, Carson started the surgery on the conjoined twins. In order to successfully operate on the twins, the team had to lower their body temperature through hypothermic and circulatory arrest. It took twenty two hours, but the operation ended successfully.

The twins were able to enjoy their lives independently after the surgery. In doing this operation, Ben Carson made medical history because it was the first time a pair of conjoined twins had been separated successfully. Nowadays, Siamese twins are separated fairly often by neurosurgeons. Dr. Carson paved the way to make the operations easier for surgeons all over the world.

The Binder twins weren't the only twins he'd separated throughout his career. In 1997, he separated a pair of type two vertical Siamese twins in South Africa. Type two vertical conjoined twins are twins who are joined at the top of the head.

It is easily one of the most difficult operations to pull off successfully without giving brain damage to at least one of the patients. With his surgical team, Ben Carson separated these twins in a twenty eight hour operation. It was the first time twins that were joined in such a way had been separated with no neurological abnormalities as a result.

Another surgical accomplishment of Carson's was an intra-uterine procedure that would relieve the pressure on a hydrocephalic fetal twin's brain. A hydrocephalic twin has water built up deep within the cavities of the brain. The only way for it to survive without acquiring massive brain damage is by draining the water via the excretory system.

Carson is also known for his hemispherectomies. These involve stopping the uncontrollable seizures an infant has due to epilepsy or some other pre-existing condition. In order to stop the seizures, half of the brain has to be removed. Even though half of the brain is gone, the other half of the brain can function just fine and actually does twice the work it would normally do without much extra effort.

These were some of his greatest career highlights and the reasons as to why Dr. Ben Carson is so highly regarded in the medical world. He has received numerous awards and honors for his work, such as the 2008 Presidential Medal of Freedom, the highest honor for any civilian in the United States. He was also chosen in 2001 by CNN and Times magazines as one of America's top physicians/scientists.

He has also been awarded at least thirty honorary doctorate degrees. The list goes on and on with the amount of honors Carson has received due to his work as a neurosurgeon.

However, being a neurosurgeon is not all life has to offer Carson. In fact, through his faith, Carson realized that he was meant to do more for this world. As an avid public speaker, Carson gathered followers as he spoke out about amendments and other policies that he believed should not be passed by the Obama administration.

He is vehemently against President Obama and in May 2015, he threw his hat into the presidential candidacy ring to vie for the nomination of the Republican Party.

4 MARRIAGE

Ben Carson met the love of his life, Lacena "Candy" Rustin, in 1971 while he attended Yale University. They married in 1975, just four years after they met.

They have been married for twenty eight years and currently have three sons. Candy and her three sons are known as the Carson Four, a rather well accomplished string quartet. The two also have grandchildren given to them by their sons.

As the first lady of the United States, Candy Carson would be expected to perform the same amount of philanthropic actions as past first ladies, such as Michelle Obama and Eleanor Roosevelt.

As people who grew up with nothing and became something, the Carson's are the type of people to give back. They even started scholarship funds for students who do well in school, regardless of their economic and religious backgrounds.

The Carsons' three sons would constantly be in the eyes of the people, should he become President of the United States. However, they are probably used to being in the public eye somewhat due to their accomplishment as a family string quartet.

Although, that is nothing in comparison to just how vicious and pervasive the paparazzi can be. If Carson becomes President, hopefully his family can handle the pressure of the situation. The responsibilities of the presidency can place a lot of stress on families.

5 WHY THE PRESIDENCY?

In order to make the world better for the grandchildren of the American people, Carson is running for President in order to give the youth of the nation a head start in life that he never head. By being charge of the educational system, he can create programs that will improve the quality of education in public schools despite the practice of common core ruling the nation.

Along with this, he will be in charge of making the economy better by implementing policies to lower the tax rate and cut government spending. With such a high national debt, it is a wonder that some would even want to be President. Having to deal with that, along with the debt ceiling, is a crisis waiting to happen.

Being President all depends on what cards you get dealt. If you are dealt a bad hand, like each President is from the President before him, then it is very hard to correct the mistakes of your predecessors. You do the best you can with what you have by working with the people in your cabinet.

No matter how many good policies one might have, if they do not have the teamwork and public speaking skills to back up their claims, then the American people will be fearful that the country will become worse off than it previously was.

Carson wants to make the people unafraid. He wants them to rely on him as President and let him use his critical thinking skills to combat problems the United States faces every day. He truly believes that as President, he can make a true difference.

He was never involved with politics prior to running for President, but he says that God called upon him to do this and that if it is His will, then so it must be.

Carson takes his faith very seriously. He believes that anything he does has to do with God's agenda. His decision to run for President of the United States was not his own doing. It is Carson's belief that God had a plan for him, which brings up the interesting question of is Carson going to be a religious preacher as President?

Will he be able to do what others in government believe should be kept separate - church and state? He didn't want to run for the presidency. In fact, the idea never really came to mind until 2013.

As he began speaking with people, especially the elderly and the young and impressionable, about United States policies, he learned that some had given up on America. Many believed that there was nothing they could do to help themselves anymore and that it was better to just wait and died than to continue hoping for a better life. Carson took all of the opinions of the people into consideration and felt compelled to begin a presidential campaign.

Although he does not have much of a political background at all, he desires to change the way politics has been forever. There is such a negative stigma regarding politics because of how many politicians tend to play dirty or turn out to be crooks. This is because the same people remain in power time and time again, even with elections.

If a neurosurgeon with no particular political streak can become president, then it is safe to say that politics may not be the answer to everything. Carson is basically insinuating that anyone should be able to run for president if they possess the problem solving and critical thinking skills necessary for success.

As a neurosurgeon, Carson had to make many decisions that were life or death for the person he was operating on. By giving directions to his team and working together to solve problems as they came up, he was able to successfully operate on his patients. This is quite like what the presidency would be like for Carson.

If he can apply his skills as a surgeon to the world of politics, then not having a background in the field shouldn't matter. So long as he has a platform and he knows how to solve problems that hardworking Americans face on a daily basis, then he deserves a shot at the presidency just as much as anyone else in the GOP does.

6 THE ISSUES

Whether you agree or disagree with Ben Carson's view on the issues facing the American people, you have to keep in mind that he is a conservative. As a republican presidential candidate, it is safe to say that his view of the issues will not differ much from his GOP opponents. However, some of his views will differ a bit from the other candidates.

On Abortion

Carson has been outspoken about how he is a pro-life supporter. In other words, he believes that the life of the fetus is precious and just as important as any other life. When it comes to abortion, he is mostly against it. He does not believe in abortion for convenience and wants to ban abortions that occur more than twenty weeks after fertilization.

As a surgeon, Carson has said that he has operated on unborn infants before and can assure the public that they are very much alive. Therefore, he believes it is wrong to take away an innocent life that cannot protect itself. The mother's decision should only be brought about by the possibility of life or death for herself. In no way, shape or form should an abortion be performed for any other reason than that the mother's life is in danger. Although, banning abortions after twenty weeks of fertilization may make it highly difficult and nearly impossible for a mother to abort her child in a life threatening emergency once she passes that mark. It is unclear whether or not Carson believes the mother's life should be protected over the infant's in this type of situation.

On the National Budget and the Economy

Carson believes in a free market and that the economy should be allowed to work its course in the way that it is supposed to. Outside government interference will cause economic turmoil to all parties involved and could result in even more economic crises in the future. He has said that 1990s deregulation is pretty much the cause of the 2008 economic crisis. Therefore, if he becomes president, he wants to cut every agency's spending by ten percent.

Ben Carson is also a supporter of a balanced budget amendment. With the national debt equaling about eighteen trillion dollars, he believes it is time for congress to pass an amendment to the constitution that will make it mandatory for the budget to be balanced at the end of each fiscal year. The national debt is the third biggest item in the federal budget with interest payments equaling about two hundred and fifty billion dollars. He has said that in order to make the future better for our grandchildren, we must ratify this amendment and make the economy better for them in the long run.

On Civil Rights

Carson has had a lot to say about civil rights in the past. Even now, although some of his ideas towards civil rights have shifted a bit due to the ever changing political agenda of the American people, he has been just as outspoken as before about human rights.

Before same-sex marriage became the law of the land, Carson believed that marriage was between one man and one woman. He also believed, and still believes, that homosexuality is a choice. He believed that those who are gay should be given rights but that they should be given the option to marry. Once same-sex marriage became the law, Carson changed his tune a little bit. Considering it is now legal for same-sex couples to marry throughout the United States, Carson agrees that since same-sex marriage is the law, it must be observed and obeyed. To this day, he still believes that homosexuality is a choice.

In regards to the political correct culture Carson despises, he has asked his followers not to listen to the "PC police" when they say conservatives are extremists. This is because the Southern Poverty Law Center put him on a list of extremists along with members of the KKK and other such groups. The SPLC apologized to Carson for labeling him as an extremist just because of his views on marriage and abortion. While people may not agree with what Carson has to say on these issues, it is rather hard to label him as an extremist because he has the right to express his views just as anyone else does.

Affirmative action, or the idea that minorities are given the benefit of the doubt and priority when it comes to things like education and job priority, is something that Carson does not like. He believes that hardworking people should work hard for what they want and need, no matter what color their skin is or what background they come from. Affirmative action was implemented in order to help those with less opportunities in a white male dominated society. Carson believes that every single person, be them minority or otherwise, has to create opportunities for themselves and work hard to earn respect and reach their goals.

On Education

As someone who lived in poverty and brought himself up through his education, Carson is a big believer in allowing schools to govern themselves. In other words, he is against common core and all that it stands for. He believes that at this point, private schooling is more beneficial than common core public schooling.

In order to better educate children, Carson set up the Carson Scholars Fund. This award is given out based on academic and humanitarian accomplishments. In order to qualify for the award, a student must have a minimum 3.75 GPA and be nominated by one of their teachers. It is an award that isn't focused on financial need or religious background. It is solely based on academic and humanitarian efforts from students in grades four through eleven.

Another initiative that the Carson Scholars Fund set up is the Ben Carson Reading Project. This program allows schools to build Ben Carson Reading Rooms – areas where children are invited to read and learn at their own leisure. Carson is an avid believer in power reading to help people obtain knowledge and build their creativity.

Ben Carson has a mnemonic device he uses when it comes to his way of life: THINK BIG. In other words, Talent, Honesty, Insight, Nice, Knowledge, Books, In-depth learning and God. The THINK BIG banner was often displayed in high schools and other public areas. The Carsons were told that they had to take these banners down because they had the word "God" on them. However, the judge ruled in their favor and they were allowed to continue displaying the banners even with the word God written on them.

The fact that school officials continuously try to ban the concept of God in their schools is one of the reasons Ben Carson has been so outspoken about "political correctness." He believes that we should leave well enough alone and allow what needs to be said, be said.

On Fossil Fuels and the Environment

In his time as president, Carson believes that the United States should continue tapping oil sources offshore and in Alaska. He thinks that if the United States has petroleum independence, then it will stop funding for terrorists in the Middle East who control our oil supply. He has no intention of stopping oil drilling and attempting to find renewable resources to use as a main energy source. This is because the climate debate is not only irrelevant to him, but distracting as well.

Even though Carson wants to continue drilling for oil and using it as a main energy source, he believes that the environment must be maintained and that it is logical to protect it for capitalists and socialists alike. It is hard to see how one can protect the environment even with oil drilling, but Carson believes that our country can both protect the environment and drill for oil without much consequence. To him, the ends justify the means and cutting off access to the Middle East is more beneficial to the nation than finding a new energy resource.

On Foreign Policy

A big talking point of the GOP is that Carson is one of the three candidates who has not held an elective office. Therefore, his take on foreign policy could be considered weak. Having visited fifty seven countries, however, Carson knows a bit more about foreign policy than some might think.

Carson is all for standing with Israel, the only democratic Middle Eastern ally of the United States. He believes that the depth and uniqueness of the bond America has with Israel is something that will never waver and must not be broken. Carson has also spoken out about an increase in jihadism in the United States over the last few years. He blames this statistic on the fact that the U.S. pulled out of Iraq. He has stated that he wants to use every resource possible to destroy the jihadists in the United States before they destroy America.

In one of the republican presidential candidate debates, Carson stated that he asked President George W. Bush not to go to war in 2003. This seemed to be a pretty ineffective talking point, but it appeared to get the attention of the people in the crowd. After this debate, because he wasn't left much room to talk about foreign policy, he wrote an op-ed wherein he discussed his take on foreign policy to the fullest extent possible. He talked about how President Obama's war on ISIS was ineffective and immoral.

Carson's war policy is that he believes the United States should be targeting the Kurds and that a war not unlike the Cold War should be waged against them. This would require propaganda and the spreading of information that originally created the fear and panic of mutually assured destruction (MAD) within the period of the Cold War.

On Gun Control

Carson is a huge supporter of the second amendment and the right to bear arms. He has said that the amendment was created with the protection of America's freedom in mind. He believes that all U.S. citizens should be able to exercise their right to carry guns without registration. Although he does not believe that the second amendment should be weakened or tampered with in any way, he does think that semi-automatic weapons should be limited to the countryside and should be carried by citizens in cities.

On Health Care

Carson has always had much to say about health care. He believes that the Affordable Care Act is an atrocity and that it was not worth the $1.2 trillion that the government spent on it. He believes that even if the Affordable Care Act continues for a good ten or so years, roughly twenty three million Americans still will not have any health insurance. He is a strong supporter of Health Savings Accounts because they protect patient freedom and choice.

On the subject of Obamacare, Carson believes that is the worst thing to happen to this country since slavery. He says that it robs people of their control and restricts them from accessing true health care services. As previously mentioned, Carson believes HSAs are the way to go. By funding these accounts from birth, they will teach the poor to use their money responsibility and teach Americans how to control their own lives.

Carson thinks parents should vaccinate their kids. He has said that there is no proven link of vaccines causing autism and that people should not be worried about that. Instead, they should be worried about the wellbeing of their children. Carson believes that vaccinations are extremely important, despite the right of an individual to refuse vaccination. He has said that some vaccines should be considered mandatory while others are given upon personal choice.

On Immigration

Carson is of the belief that deportation is the low moral road for immigration in the United States. Instead of building a wall to keep immigrants out after deporting the majority of them, he wants to initiate a guest worker program. This is taking a page out of Canada's book, wherein their guest worker program allows people to enter the country as a guest worker, but makes them pay taxes and receive benefits. They are free to come and go from the country as they please without infringing on anybody's rights.

Is it fair to use illegal immigrants as cheap labor and deny them citizenship? Carson has said that a huge portion of the American economy would collapse without undocumented workers. People use the illegal labor and abuse it while continuing to harass and discuss the deportation of the very people who do their labor. The guest worker program will hopefully solve these issues and stop illegal immigration.

On Crime and Drugs

Carson has said that there appears to be a politically correct prejudice against blacks versus whites and he wants it to stop. He has said of the Trayvon Martin case that although the justice system is flawed, it is the best system that the United States has. As a result, Carson has said that perhaps equipping police with body cameras will avoid their use of excessive force and abuse of power.

On the topic of drugs, Carson never really got into the 1960s sex and drugs crowd. This was because of his religion. Practicing his faith kept him away from the growing party trend of the 1960s. Carson is an advocator of medical marijuana for patients who are in dire need of it, but not as a leisurely pastime.

The recreational use of marijuana is wrong in his eyes. He has also stated the lowering the blood alcohol from .08 to .02 will reduce the amount of drunk driving on the streets.

On Government Reform

Carson has spoken up about why the government needs to take a step back and look at itself from the eyes of the people. He believes that there are way too many government officials and that the government keeps itself busy for the sake of justifying its existence.

In order to decrease the number of people directly involved with government decision making processes, Carson thinks that House terms should be extended to six to ten years with no re-election at the end of the term. This will limit the number of government officials in the House.

According to Carson, there is a surplus of lawyers in the government, but not enough doctors. Considering he himself is a doctor, it is only logical that he would advocate for more doctors to be involved in the government. With their critical thinking and problem solving skills, doctors are wonderful candidates for government jobs.

Carson believes that it is human nature that makes giving up power difficult. Therefore, government officials are power hungry and re-election is a way for them to retain their power for a longer period of time. Carson has said that there should be a five year hiring freeze in order to limit and decrease the number of government officials. Decreasing the size of the government is the best way for free market enterprises and self-regulation of the economy to work its course.

On Homeland Security

The United States military is at the smallest it has ever been, according to Ben Carson. Therefore, fighting back is harder than it might seem. It is bad to tie the hands of the military and not allow them to fight back against terrorists.

Carson realizes that ISIS is a clear threat to the American people and that in order to get rid of them, measures must be taken to ensure total destruction of the organization.

Carson believes that if you use ethical world leadership, then it will be easier to stop the "bullies" of the world. In this case, Iran and other surrounding Middle Eastern countries would be considered the bullies. Carson has said that Shia-led Iran is even more dangerous than ISIS. In other words, Carson's take on homeland security is that the threats need to be taken out before the homeland itself is taken out.

On Jobs

Although Carson hasn't been a strong advocate for raising the minimum wage, he does agree that the minimum wage should probably be raised and then indexed. He has also stated that unions are bad when they hold too much power. They should focus on the future of the next generation rather than using the power they have now to further themselves as individuals.

On Tax Reform

Due to the fact that the bible supports a flat tax, Carson has said that keeping a flat tax with a ten percent tithing rate is the best way to start a tax reformation process. If there is a proportional tithe system, then the IRS will not be needed. This would make taxation much easier in Carson's eyes and better for the United States as a whole.

Carson is a firm believer that wealth should not be redistributed from the wealthy to the poor. He does not believe that anything is wrong with the rich finding loopholes and using them to their advantage.

He does not want to put a progressive taxation on the rich because that is socialism. As most people know, republicans and conservatives generally do not agree with socialism. Carson is no exception.

On Welfare and Poverty

Carson wants to get rid of dependency in order to be compassionate towards those who are suffering on welfare and in poverty. By making education accessible to the needy and requiring them to work, poverty can be eradicated.

Those who do not want to work will not get any help from the government. Carson believes that charities, especially private-sector charities, do a better job at helping those in need than the government does.

He has been known to say that those who use welfare are lazy. Much like with affirmative action, welfare is something used to give opportunities to the less fortunate. People tend to abuse it, though, giving everyone on welfare a bad reputation as a result. Instead of calling out those who abuse welfare, Carson, like most people, group people that use welfare in with those who abuse it.

On Guantanamo Bay

In Carson's eyes, it is beneficial to keep Gitmo open. By keeping the detention facility open, the United States will be safer from terrorist attacks and prevent another catastrophe like 9/11 from occurring. Gitmo is responsible for trapping radical terrorists and containing tem until their trial by military commission is granted. According to Carson, Gitmo is by far the most convenient and safest facility to detain these radicals.

On Russia

Russia's newfound aggression under President Vladimir Putin is something that Carson cannot allow. In order to combat Russia's transgressions upon other countries such as Ukraine and those in the Middle East, the United States of America must lead NATO and non-NATO allies in a position wherein they can protect themselves and also take an offensive against the aggressive country. In other words, Carson would like to relay to Putin just how dire the consequences will be if any transgressions are made upon the United States and her allies.

Although these aren't all of the issues Ben Carson has a position on, they are the ones he has made crucial to his campaign.

7 THE GOOD

To most, it seems like Ben Carson has the passion befitting of a President. He truly wants what is best for America, even if some of his policies may seem like they are not reflecting that fact. This is what Carson believes will truly help America grow and prosper. There is no ulterior motive or anything behind his run for the candidacy. He believes that is God's plan to have him run for President.

The fact that Carson has never held an office before is a double-edged sword. The good part about it is that he is a unique candidate in most aspects. He uses his background as a surgeon in order to come up with plausible solutions to complex problems.

Even though he touts his religion in most issues, he has stayed relatively firm with his beliefs. Consistency is something that people, especially voters, like to see. If a candidate changes their ideas because they don't seem to be favorable in the eyes of the people, it seems like the candidate is selling out. Carson is obviously not a sellout.

The Conservative View

In terms of the pro-life debate, Carson's view is spot on. Most conservatives are of the belief that abortions for convenience should not be allowed and that the fetus should be protected at all costs. After all, a fetus is a life just like any other. A twenty week abortion period is too much for most conservatives, but it is a good medium to give the woman an out if she is having a difficult or life threatening pregnancy.

On the topic of immigration, illegal immigrants should not be allowed into the country. Hardworking Americans whose families have lived her for decades should have the same opportunities as past generations have had. Therefore, decreasing the population by deporting immigrants is the way to go.

However, Carson doesn't believe that. He believes in having guest worker permits for immigrants who have not yet become citizens in the country. This is a fair deal because immigrants who work here won't be increasing the population and the country as a whole will not be forced to speak another language against its own will.

Most conservatives are not in favor of raising the minimum wage because they believe that minimum wage jobs are not to be used to raise families with. They are for college students and jobs that one would have while looking for other work. Spending money is acquired through minimum wage jobs.

Although, many people do work minimum wage jobs to feed their families. If the minimum wage is raised, then hours will be cut and less people will be put to work. Carson finds a good medium between the two in saying that the minimum wage should be raised and then indexed (adjusted to inflation). This means that even if the price index rises, minimum wage will continue to provide the same monetary value as minimum wage prior to inflation.

Keeping Gitmo open is definitely a good idea for Carson to expand upon. It is with the American peoples' safety in mind that Guantanamo Bay stays open and continues to isolate terrorists from the rest of the world. It is working to keep the facility open that is going to be difficult, but if anyone can do it, Carson seems to think he can.

On the issue of foreign policy, Russia's transgression needs to be stopped before it begins. Carson is right when he says that America needs to show Putin who is boss. Whenever one of America's allies is attacked, the country has to fight right back.

Waiting for aggression, instead of standing up to it immediately, will only make things worse. The same goes for the enemies the United States has in other countries and the Middle East. The idea of nuclear war cannot simply be stopped by a nuclear war pact with a Middle Eastern country. The agreement will not last forever and once the pact is over, there is only so much time before an offensive is taken against America.

Carson's political standpoints are very much traditional Republican views. Although the other candidates might have slightly differing viewpoints, they all stay within the same target realm. In the pro-life versus pro-choice argument, Republicans almost always take the pro-life route. This is because traditional conservative ideologies brought them up with the idea that a fetus is as much a person as the mother it is growing inside of.

Regarding immigration, most conservatives think it is unfair to have illegal immigrants in America when other immigrants who have been waiting years to become citizens in this country get cut in line. In regards to religion, most Republicans bring their religion into their politics, especially those who practice the Catholic faith. No matter what, God has to be a part of their campaign.

Carson incorporates all of these traditional conservative ideas into his campaign platform in order to ensure the majority of the conservative vote in the nomination for the Republican candidacy.

The Liberal View

Carson has a pretty favorable view on the topic of education. Most people in the nation have not had any favorable things to say about common core. Although the idea of private schooling may seem expensive, private schools retain the traditional way of teaching and do not adhere to common core public school practices. Carson is definitely right when he says that common core is something that has to go. This is an idea that is pretty universal across party lines.

Ben Carson is also an incredible public speaker. Much like President Obama, he has the social skills to be a truly great politician. He has inspired audiences of thousands of people to stand and rally with him as the next republican presidential candidate.

Through public speaking and having one-on-one conversations with his supporters, he was able to realize that the next step in his life was going to be to vie for the republican nomination for President of the United States.

Although Carson believes that homosexuality is a choice, he upholds the fact that same-sex marriage is now the law of the land. The fact that he will not combat this issue is rather admirable of him. He had the belief for the longest time that same-sex marriage should not be upheld in a court of law, but now that it is law, it must be observed.

A balanced budget amendment is something that people in the United States have been waiting for since the national debt began piling up again under President Bush. Carson has the favorable view when he says that the government should be forced to wipe out the national debt through an amendment to the constitution.

This could cause problems down the line, but the fact of the matter is that the national debt will never be wiped out if necessary steps and sacrifices aren't made to prevent an even wider margin between a potentially balanced budget and the deficit.

Carson's view on immigration is rather favorable in the eyes of liberals. Rather than kicking all of the immigrants out, having a guest worker program is a great alternative. This type of program has been proven to work, seeing as how Canada implemented the idea and it has worked out rather well.

To deny immigrants citizenship after they came here and worked undocumented for a meager amount of pay is atrocious, so allowing them to work here and come and go as they please while their citizenship is pending is a good way to go.

8 THE BAD

There are many things that could be considered poor views on several of the issues Ben Carson is passionate about. He is not a bad candidate for the presidency, but some of his policies could make him an unfavorable President in the future. Even though Carson is ahead in the polls at the time this book was written, that could easily change with time. He has to keep strong to his views if he wants to continue gaining voters. If he changes his views to appeal to certain crowds, he could be labeled as a sellout.

The Conservative View

The idea of same-sex marriage is considered a sin in the eyes of God, according to most conservatives. Although religion should not be a factor in deciding a person's way of life, many conservatives would agree that homosexuality is, in fact, a choice.

However, that doesn't make same-sex marriage okay and it doesn't mean they have to observe it. The fact that Carson won't fight the court decision of same-sex marriage is a turn off to many voters, especially in more conservative parts of the country.

There are many people, like the Kim Davis' of the world, who would agree that recognizing same-sex marriage is immoral if you are a catholic and, under the word of God, it does not have to be recognized.

Conservatives also generally believe that big government is helpful in regulating the economy. Governments should have many officials to make project planning and job distribution easier. Despite the fact that the officials could do nothing all year and still get large paychecks, having more Republican officials in the House makes it easier to get Republicans voted in.

Along with this, free markets are not always successful. Having the economy regulate itself has done damage in the past and, with the way the economy is now, it would not do good to allow it to rest itself. Something has to be done to make the economy better and fast. Waiting for the business cycle to go about again without getting the government involved is a bad idea on Carson's part.

From the conservative point of view, it is hard to find many flaws in Carson's ideas and platforms. Mostly everything follows traditional Republican views, despite a few differences in points of view on marriage and government.

Overall, Carson is a very good Republican candidate and appeals to the conservative crowd very well. He will be a hard candidate to beat in debates when it comes to talking about the real issues and how to solve them. As a critical thinker, it is Carson's natural talent to come up with solutions to complex problems.

The Liberal View

In the film *Gifted Hands: The Ben Carson Story*, Carson is made out to be some superhero being who became a fantastic neurosurgeon. What it doesn't show you, however, is just how bad many of his political views are. He is a great doctor, but he definitely needs some work as a politician. This just goes to show how our perception of a person can be skewed after they step into the political ring.

Politics can create a whole new person out of someone. In fact, it has even ruined some people beyond all rhyme or reason. Politics is a nasty game that requires the best of the best to step into the ring and fight it out with the other politicians. Carson just does not have the experience to be as great of a politician as he thinks he is.

His views on abortion alienate women and their rights. Even though he has a more lenient view towards allowing abortion for a twenty week period after fertilization, not allowing late term abortions for women who will die otherwise seems to be quite inhumane. It is one thing to have an abortion for convenience, but it is another thing altogether to have to abort because you are in a life or death situation.

Along with his views on abortion, his views on gay marriage also aren't within the liberal standpoint. For example, even though he agrees that same-sex marriage is the law of the land, he did not endorse gay couples prior to the court decision.

He also believes that homosexuality is a choice. In all actuality, homosexuality has been proven scientifically to not be a choice. Not only is Carson wrong in this aspect, but it also makes his science background look rather dis-credible.

Socialism is something that most conservatives tend to abhor. Carson has stated that he is not a socialist and that he does not believe in re-distributing wealth among people of different economic statuses. To liberals, this would seem like a rather skewed point of view. How can you strengthen the lower and middle classes if you won't tax the rich?

Carson's idea of tithing and having a flat tax rate would seem to be the way to go in this situation. However, if it were possible to save the economy by doing this, wouldn't it have been done already? Carson says that he started to become a republican after listening to Reagan. Reaganomics, while good in theory, hasn't actually proven itself to be the way to go. Some say that Reagan got lucky during his term and that is why Reaganomics was successful. Therefore, in a time of such economic crisis and a national debt of $1.2 trillion, it is hard to believe that a flat tax would work.

On the discussion of homeland security and how it should be approached, Carson has done a bad job with handling his viewpoints on this. Most conservatives just want to crush the opposition rather than negotiating with them. Obama's nuclear war deal was rather successful and although the looming threat of terrorism isn't gone, the negotiations we have had with the Middle East point towards a more promising future.

George Washington told the United States to stay out of foreign affairs in the first place. However, foreign policy is such a vital part of the American economic state that it is sort of impossible not to get involved in affairs overseas. If U.S. allies are being attacked, it is the American peoples' job to help them out so that they can continue to help the United States in the future.

Although Carson is against affirmative action, he is actually a direct product of it. Affirmative action is what helped him get into Yale and allowed him to succeed in everything he did as a result. Even though his grades were good, it is no secret that minority students are given priority over the majority.

Having a diverse cultural background in schools, especially schools as prestigious as the Ivy leagues, is important in continuing to acquire the funds they receive directly from the government.

Along with this, Carson has stated that those on welfare are lazy and that they should help themselves. However, his family lived on welfare for quite a few years. He grew up in poverty and rose up due to the help of welfare, hard work and affirmative action, not all of them weighing the same amount in his life. It is rather hypocritical for Carson to condemn both affirmative action and welfare when he himself used both in his lifetime.

It is understandable that because he no longer needs these two things that he is looking down on them in retrospect and hindsight, but the fact of the matter is that he should be compassionate towards those who are in the same spot he was when he was younger. To condemn them and call these people lazy is to, in fact, call himself lazy.

Carson's hypocrisy and religious background is much of the reason why his viewpoints tend to be seen as controversial. With God always in the picture and Carson's past always lurking in the rearview mirror, it is hard not to talk about the flaws of each of his campaign ideas.

He is one of the more honest candidates in the GOP and he has more integrity than most, but can the American people trust someone who would condemn those living in poverty simply because they cannot help it?

Carson seems to think that being poor is a choice and that you can always get yourself out of poverty if you try hard enough. This isn't the case because of the current economic crisis. Although the job market is getting better under Obama, that doesn't mean it is easy to get a job without a college degree and no money with which to go to college to get said degree.

It is incredibly hard to get out of poverty and work yourself from the ground up in this kind of economy. Carson believes that getting rid of dependency shows true compassion, but how can you get rid of dependency if you don't re-distribute wealth from the rich and give it to poor?

This is not to say that all poor people should be given free money. In fact, there should be a background check involved and forms and the whole nine yards because free money is, in fact, free money. Welfare is considered to be a free money program, but it would be so much more beneficial if it actually gave people a wage amount that could help further their existence.

Food stamps cover groceries and welfare covers rent, utilities and bills. If there are but sixty dollars left over, how is that supposed to get anyone anywhere? Depending on the city the person lives in, that amount would probably not even cover the transportation it would take going from company to company looking for a job.

To have lived on welfare and taken advantage of affirmative action only to condemn it later on in life is hypocritical of Carson, but perhaps he just wants a better life for the American people than he had when he was growing up. He probably did not like being on welfare and although affirmative action helped further his schooling and career, he wanted to make it on his own without help from other people. This is where his strong character and integrity comes from. Being a self-made man really looks good in the eyes of the people.

Looking at Carson's platform from a liberal point of view definitely puts a very different spin on things. Since Carson is a Republican and a conservative, it is safe to assume that liberals think that he is bad news. The same is true of conservatives when talking about liberal, Democratic candidates.

A middle ground is hard to find between the two parties, which is why some candidates go independent. Although not much information has been given about the independent candidates this year, they will not be much of a match against what the Republican and Democratic parties have to offer in terms of candidates this year.

9 THE ELECTION

As the 2016 presidential election draws near, it is easy to see that Ben Carson has his work cut out for him. While his platform is clear and he has done rather well in the GOP debates, his opponents are more qualified than him on the political spectrum. It is a wonder whether or not his inexperience will get the best of him or if it will be a plus.

People don't like change, but with the type of state the United States is currently in, something is going to have to give. Perhaps the nation needs someone with the critical thinking skills Carson possesses. Anyone is eligible to become the President of the United States so long as they were born there. Why, then, should Carson not be taken seriously as a candidate?

Carson has all of the public speaking skills necessary for a political office. He is also fantastic at assessing damage and working towards a logical solution to the problem. These are the types of skills one needs to possess as the President.

Should someone like Donald Trump, who builds his image upon his billion dollar empire, be considered a better candidate than a local surgeon who has listened to the concerns of the people, taken them into consideration and come up with logical solutions based upon the current state of the union?

One of the downfalls of Carson is just how much he brings his faith into his political discussions. The concept of separation of church and state still rings true to this very day. Religion, while important, should not be something used as a way to get the vote of the people. The President of the United States is supposed to be Protestant.

While Carson is allowed to be Catholic, having such a religion alienates those who are not of the same faith. It is definitely difficult for those who do not follow the Catholic faith to relate to Carson's views when he credits most of his success and opinions to what God has taught him. This is exactly why most presidents have been of the Protestant faith.

Presidential candidates have to be able to handle the hard questions. If a candidate says they can stare down opposing countries and they aren't afraid to fight the "good fight," then they cannot be afraid of having tough questions thrown at them by the very people who are voting for them to be elected. Carson has done an excellent job of answering questions in the GOP debates, even though his answers were, at times, rather vague.

However, penning an entire op-ed on his take on foreign policy because he wasn't really given a chance to weigh in on the subject during the second Republican debate was a good move in showing that he truly cares about the people having full access to his knowledge and policies. Due to his performance in the second debate, he is now up in the polls in front of Donald Trump.

Donald Trump seems to be the one candidate that Carson is truly going to have a tough time defeating in the primaries. Trump is a very popular candidate not only due to his controversial campaigning style, but also because many people, especially older people, agree with his ideas.

Although building a wall to keep immigrants out probably is not the best way to go about handling the immigration issue facing this country, it is something that the American people haven't heard before and want to cling onto. New ideas are what keep people interested. In order to defeat Trump, Carson just has to keep on doing what he's been doing, which is besting all of the other candidates in the GOP debates.

Regardless of how you look at it, pretty much every candidate sans two has more experience than Ben Carson in the political arena. Donald Trump has even said that Carson just does not have the experience necessary in order to become President.

However, the reason why Carson is so popular is because he is the outsider candidate. While both he and Trump built themselves from the ground up, Carson is the one who has the least political experience. While he has been given numerous awards, including the Presidential Medal of Freedom, he is lesser known than most of the other candidates in the race.

The fact that he skyrocketed past Trump to lead the polls isn't really a miracle. It just means that Trump's campaign style is starting to frizzle out.

Trump's tactic is to say that he is going to make America great again because he can. Carson has solutions and reasons to back up every single one of the decisions he wants to make as the next President. People are tired of hearing Trump's same old song and dance over and over again.

Every time Carson speaks, he has something new to offer – something fresh. Donald Trump is the most widely known candidate in this race. This is both a blessing and a curse because although Trump was wildly popular at first, everyone knows what he is about now. If he doesn't ever have anything new to offer, then he becomes old news really fast.

Candidates like Marco Rubio, Jeb Bush and Ted Cruz have a slim chance of getting a poll boost before the primaries, but chances are that Carson and Trump will dominate the polls during the primaries. It will most definitely be one of these two who becomes the next GOP candidate for President of the United States.

It all comes down to who has the better campaign platform and ideas in the eyes of the American people. As of right now, it seems as if the odds are in Carson's favor.

Unlike Hilary Clinton, Ben Carson has the backing of people based on honesty and integrity. Carson appears to be a very honest man whereas Clinton's email scandals have given her a bad rep with voters all over the country. Should Clinton be Carson's opponent after the primaries, then it would probably be a gridlock fight to the finish.

This is because although Clinton is funded by big corporations and she does not seem to be very relatable to either Republicans or Democrats, she has the experience of being Secretary of State and several other political offices under her belt. On top of this, her husband was President of the United States, so she also has the experience of serving as the First Lady.

Should Bernie Sanders become Carson's opponent once the primaries are over, then Carson has a new hurdle to climb over. Sanders' flaw is that he appeals mostly to the younger audiences. However, this could also be considered a Trump card. Carson appeals to the older generation, as most Republicans tend to.

The newer generation is more liberal and democratic than ever before and while it is not rare to find young Republicans, it is certainly rare to find a handful of one hundred random kids who are Republican by majority. Carson probably won't be getting the majority of the younger vote, but if he can grab the attention of the middle aged to the elderly, then he's got a great deal of baby boomers to work with.

Both Sanders and Clinton tend not to bring religion into politics. In fact, none of the Democratic candidates really do. This is both an advantage and a disadvantage for Carson. While he can use his religion to continue appealing to the older generations and their religious practices, he also cannot relate religiously to those who are not of his faith.

It almost seems as if his political platform is aimed solely towards Catholics, even though that is not the case. The Democratic Party also tends to have one thing the GOP does not, and that is the LGBT vote. LGBT people make up a larger percentage of the population than ever before due to social stigmas being taken away left and right.

They show up in statistics more often because there are less closeted individuals and more registered gay voters. Most GOP candidates do not agree with same-sex marriage even though it has become the law of the land. Therefore, LGBT voters tend to favor the Democratic Party. This could potentially contain from five to ten percent of the votes cast during the Presidential election. That could mean the difference between winning or losing the presidency for Carson and Trump.

The primary elections begin next year. You can find a full list of voting dates for each state online. It is incredibly important to vote because you never really know which candidate is the actual favorite until the results of the elections are released to the public. Whether you love him or you hate him, Ben Carson has built an image for himself from the ground up. From not wanting to campaign for President of the United States to going into full on campaign mode with a platform and everything, it is clear to see that Carson has truly prepared for this. Whether or not he is ready for the responsibility of having this position is up to you, the voter, to decide.

ABOUT THE AUTHOR

Michael Joshua got his undergraduate degree in Finance and works full time at a large bank as a Financial Analyst. He has great knowledge in Business & Money, along with politics and technology.

Goodreads:

https://www.goodreads.com/user/show/46377085-michael-joshua

Twitter:

https://twitter.com/mjoshua_author

www.ingramcontent.com/pod-product-compliance
Lightning Source LLC
Chambersburg PA
CBHW071137280526
45787CB00003B/1315